FRANK DABBA SMITH was born in California. He studied
Linguistic Anthropology at the University of California in Berkeley,
and became a teacher. In 1994 he was ordained as a rabbi
at Leo Baeck College, London. Dabba Smith also works as a freelance
photographer, and *The Economist* has published over 150 of his images.
Frank's first book for Frances Lincoln was *My Secret Camera*.

For Cathy, Miriam, Lewis and Sarah

The author is grateful to: Dr Knut Kühn-Leitz, Barbara Kühn-Leitz, Johanna Leitz,
Henri Cartier-Bresson, Rabbi Alexander Dukhovny, Doris Ebertz, Walter Ebertz, Henry Ebner,
Rina Eilon, Gideon Fiegel, Cathy Fischgrund, Rolf Fricke, Rabbi Albert Friedlander,
Evelyn Friedlander, George Gilbert, Malcolm Hart, Dr Gwilym Hughes, Jan Jaben-Eilon,
Berthe Krull, Alexandra Kuzmenko, Norman Lipton, Gisela Lonkwitz, John Morris, Leon Morris,
Rabbi Jeffrey Newman, Sophie Pelham, Susan Posner, Gemma Rochelle, Paul Rosenthal,
Josephine W. Smith (z"l), M. David Smith (z"l), Helen Wright and Victoria Zackheim.

The abbreviation (z"l) refers to the Hebrew wording for 'of blessed memory'.

First published in Great Britain in 2003 by
Frances Lincoln Children's Books, 4 Torriano Mews,
Torriano Avenue, London NW5 2RZ

www.franceslincoln.com

First paperback edition 2006

Distributed in the USA by Publishers Group West

British Library Cataloguing in Publication Data available on request

ISBN 1-84507-006-2

Printed in Singapore
1 3 5 7 9 8 6 4 2

elsie's war

a story of courage in nazi germany

frank dabba smith

introduction by henri cartier-bresson

FRANCES LINCOLN

I knew Elsie Leitz well and she always welcomed me warmly

to Haus Friedwart when I visited Wetzlar.

I was very impressed by her passionate concern for

international humanitarian causes, and by the great risks

she took during the war to save many people who were

in danger.

I remember her with deep admiration.

Henri Cartier-Bresson

J'ai bien connu Elsie Leitz
qui m'a toujours reçu Hans
Friedwart très chaleureuse-
ment pendant mes séjours à
Wetzlar.

J'étais très impressionné
par ses profondes préoccupa-
tions pour les causes hu-
manitaires internationales,
et les grands risques qu'elle
a couru en sauvant de
nombreuses personnes mena-
cées pendant la guerre.

Je salue profondément
sa mémoire.

Henri Cartier-Bresson
(Leicaiste amateur)

ELSIE KÜHN-LEITZ AND HER FAMILY lived in Germany during
the Second World War.

This war was one of the most deadly ever to be fought.
The Nazis took control of Germany and they wanted to get rid
of everyone they disagreed with or simply didn't like.
They imprisoned many innocent people in concentration camps,
where conditions were unspeakable and millions were murdered.

Elsie and her family hated what the Nazis were doing
and Elsie spent the war struggling for freedom and justice
for those in danger.

This is Elsie's story.

Elsie Kühn-Leitz

WHEN THE NAZIS FIRST CAME TO POWER in 1933, they started to make life very difficult for many German citizens. Jewish people especially were bullied and beaten up. Anyone who disagreed with the Nazis' cruel ideas was put in jail and often would be killed.

Elsie's father owned the Leitz camera factory in Wetzlar, near Frankfurt. As soon as he realised that Jewish people were in danger from the Nazis, he began to give many young Jews work in the factory. Here, they received the help that allowed them to escape Nazi Germany and find good jobs abroad, in safety and freedom.

A Nazi rally in the main square, Wetzlar

AFTER THE WAR BEGAN IN 1939, Leitz could no longer sell their famous products around the world. The Nazis demanded instead that Leitz make cameras, binoculars and other equipment to help them in the war.

The factory had lost many workers who had gone to fight as soldiers. So the Nazis sent Ukrainian women to work as slaves, and they were trained to do some of the work in the factory.

Elsie wanted to do something to help these people, who were so far from their homes and families.

The Leitz factory

ELSIE GAVE THE WORKERS EXTRA FOOD, blankets and clothing... even radios.

One of the young women, Nina Bezzubenko, spent long hours in the factory polishing lenses. The work was very hard, but thanks to Elsie her life was a bit more comfortable.

The Gestapo (the dreaded Nazi police) would be furious if they found out that Elsie was helping these women. But Elsie's greatest challenge of all was yet to come: a challenge that would put her very life in danger.

In May 1943, she was asked to help a Jewish lady, Hedwig Palm, to flee to Switzerland. Hedwig had to escape, as the Gestapo were coming to take her away to a concentration camp where she would surely die.

Elsie made secret plans, arranging for Hedwig to go and hide at the home of Elsie's aunt in Munich, near Switzerland. From here she could journey across the Swiss border to freedom.

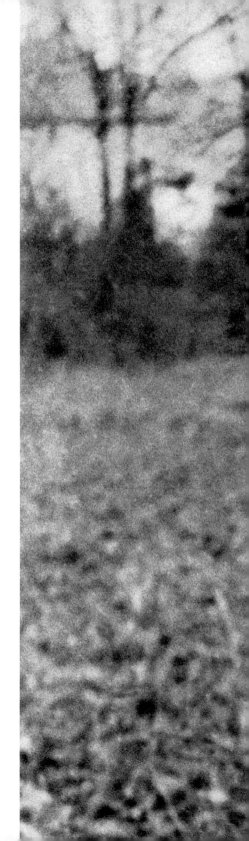

Nina Bezzubenko (right) and friend
(the word 'Ost' sewn on the jacket shows them
to be forced workers from Eastern Europe)

Kennort:	*Wetzlar*
Rennummer:	*A 0011*
Gültig bis	*1. März* 19*44*
Name	*Berliner* *geb. Schreiner*
Vornamen	*Johanna* *Sara*
Geburtstag	*31. Oktober 1888*
Geburtsort	*Osnabrück*
Beruf	*ohne*
Unveränderliche Rennzeichen	
Veränderliche Rennzeichen	*Brille*
Bemerkungen:	*Witwe*

(Unterschrift des ...)

......, den ...

Der ...

als ...

HEDWIG SET OFF IN THE DEAD OF NIGHT, terrified for her life, sure that at any moment her identity card would be demanded. If anyone found out that she was Jewish, all would be lost.

At last, she arrived safely at the home of Elsie's aunt. But the next step was going to be even more dangerous.

After hiding for a few weeks, Hedwig set off again towards Switzerland. Although Elsie had given her a map, she grew tired and confused, and soon she was quite lost.

She hailed a passing milk truck and asked the driver for directions, praying that she could trust him. Surely she would be able to cross safely, now.

But the driver had guessed that Hedwig was Jewish; without hesitation, he betrayed her to the border police.

Elsie's plan had failed.

Hedwig Palm's identity card
(the large 'J' on the left shows that she is Jewish)

THE GESTAPO SOON FOUND OUT that Elsie had helped Hedwig. They summoned her to their offices in Wetzlar.

Now it was Elsie's turn to be afraid for her life. "I could not but fear the worst for myself," she said.

The Gestapo questioned her harshly for many hours. Then came the words which she had been dreading: "You are under arrest."

Elsie was escorted home to say farewell to her family. Her children were getting ready for bed when she came to say goodbye. She would never forget their anxious faces when she told them she was going away.

"I'll be back home in a few days," she said, trying to sound cheerful; she knew she might never see them again.

Elsie with her children, Cornelia and Knut

ELSIE WAS IMPRISONED in the Gestapo jail in Frankfurt. Her tiny cell was filthy. Her eyes burned and streamed with tears from trying to read in the darkness. Her skin itched from the bugs. Everything stank. She was lonely and afraid, but she struggled to feel free in her heart.

Elsie's jail on Klapperfeld Strasse in Frankfurt

AS TIME DRAGGED ON, Elsie grew weaker and weaker. Sometimes she was allowed to receive small packages of food from her father.

"I shared these goodies with my comrades, all of whom were as hungry as I," she said.

She tried to be cheerful and strong so that she could be a support to the other women in the jail. To keep up her spirits, she sometimes stood on a small stool in her cell and watched glimmers of sunlight coming through the tiny window. To keep up her strength, she did daily gymnastics, finishing with a handstand against the heavily-locked door.

And Elsie gained strength from her fellow prisoners, too. She made friends with Thusnelda, who was old and ill.

"Young lady, never despair!" urged Thusnelda. "The door which opened to admit you to this place will open again to free you."

Inside the Klapperfeld Strasse jail

THUSNELDA WAS RIGHT. Elsie was luckier than most of the other prisoners – her life was saved. With the help of a friend, her father paid the Gestapo a ransom so that she could be released.

"I cannot find words to describe my feeling of happiness over my new-found freedom," she declared.

When she arrived home, Elsie crawled up the front steps on her knees, grateful that she had lived to see her family again. Her father had become ill with worry during her absence. He seemed to have aged many years. Now it was Elsie's turn to care for him.

Elsie with her father, Dr Ernst Leitz II

AS THE WAR CONTINUED, Elsie's health slowly recovered. The Gestapo never stopped watching her and often they summoned her for questioning.

At last, in March 1945, American soldiers were on their way to liberate Wetzlar. Elsie jumped on her bicycle, hoping to meet the American commanders. She had to make several detours to avoid being seen by the few remaining German soldiers. At last she found an American officer and assured him that the people of Wetzlar would not resist their arrival.

As the tanks rolled into the town to free its citizens from the Nazis, she watched with tears in her eyes.

Elsie's war was over.

American tanks arrive outside the Leitz factory

The text of *Elsie's War* maintains the spirit of the post-war writings of Elsie Kühn-Leitz (1903-1985), in which she described her war-time activities.

According to Elsie's account, her final words to the Gestapo interrogators before losing her freedom on 9 September 1943 were, "It was the law of humanitarianism which provoked me into acting as I did and I felt no reason for regret." In her testimony, her humanitarian values emerge. She had a respect for all human beings, regardless of background; a profound sense of justice; a determination to do what is right and to help others; and a willingness to act spontaneously and to shoulder risks.

Elsie inherited her values from her father, Dr Ernst Leitz II (1871-1956), the owner of the world-renowned Leitz optical works in Wetzlar, Germany. Leitz was particularly respected for making the Leica, the world's first successful 35mm camera.

Elsie remained devoted to her famous father until the end of his long and extraordinarily productive life. Unfortunately her own mother, Elsie Gürtler, died in 1910. Although Elsie's marriage to Kurt Kühn ended in divorce, she bore three children: Knut, Cornelia and Karin.

The Leitz family firm had long been recognised for its positive paternal outlook towards employees. According to refugees and eyewitnesses, the company began helping numerous Jewish people, starting within days of when the Nazi nightmare began in 1933. Young Jews were offered lengthy contracts as apprentices in Wetzlar; their passages to safety in America were later arranged and subsidised. Others, who ran camera shops in Germany, were also assisted when escaping abroad. These activities posed considerable risks for the Leitz family, both in terms of their personal welfare and the continuation of their business.

Leitz was compelled to supply optical equipment to the German military, despite having lost a great number of workers to the war. In 1942, 700-800 Ukrainian women were sent to the factory as forced labourers. Elsie was very concerned with improving the day-to-day conditions of these women and her activities aroused the suspicions of the Gestapo.

In 1943, Elsie was imprisoned by the secret police for her role in the attempted escape of a Wetzlar Jewish woman, Hedwig Palm, to Switzerland. Threatened with deportation to the concentration camp Ravensbrück, Elsie was only saved by a massive ransom negotiated by an influential family friend, Dr Willi Hof.

After the war, she became deeply involved in supporting Dr Albert Schweitzer's activities to bring physical healing to Africa. She also worked tirelessly with Chancellor Konrad Adenauer in promoting Germany's efforts to reconcile with other nations, especially France.

In Elsie Kühn-Leitz we clearly see a courageous woman, motivated throughout her life by the stirring of her heart to help others in distress. By studying the lives and actions of individuals such as this, we may be inspired to act as rescuers, even in the darkest of times.

Elsie Kühn-Leitz's account of her imprisonment is included with other letters and experiences in *Elsie Kühn-Leitz Mut Zur Menschlichkeit, Vom Wirken einer Frau in ihrer Zeit*, edited by Dr Klaus Otto Nass and published by Europa Union Verlag in 1994; 521 pages; ISBN 3-7713-0451-4.

MORE PICTURE BOOKS IN PAPERBACK FROM FRANCES LINCOLN

MY SECRET CAMERA
Life in the Lodz Ghetto
Frank Dabba Smith
Photographs by Mendel Grossman

Mendel Grossman, a talented young photographer imprisoned in Lodz,
secretly produced photographs of the Ghetto documenting the horrors
of the Nazi regime. This is a book to inspire and educate.

THE VANISHING RAINFOREST
Richard Platt
Illustrated by Rupert van Wyk

Why is the Brazilian rainforest vanishing so fast? This story, seen through
the eyes of a child called Remaema, describes how the Yanomami tribe
are still battling against potential developers. Can a solution be found
that will protect the forest and allow the tribe to preserve their way of life?

PETAR'S SONG
Pratima Mitchell
Illustrated by Caroline Binch

Petar loves music, but when war breaks out Petar, his mother, brother
and sister have to leave their valley and cross the border to safety, leaving
their father behind. Petar misses his father so badly that he cannot
play his violin – until one day a song of peace comes into his head.

Frances Lincoln titles are available from all good bookshops.
You can also buy books and find out more about your favourite titles, authors and illustrators
on our website: **www.franceslincoln.com**